Songs That Made America

By the same author

The Quiet Land
The Gentle People: A Portrait of the Amish

Songs That Made America

James Warner

Grossman Publishers　　New York　　1972

Copyright © 1972 by James A. Warner
All rights reserved
First published in 1972 by Grossman Publishers
625 Madison Avenue, New York, N.Y. 10022
Published simultaneously in Canada by
Fitzhenry and Whiteside, Ltd.
SBN 670-65757-3
Library of Congress Catalogue Card Number: 72-77706
Printed in U.S.A.

Acknowledgment and warm thanks are due to John Mitchum for his long hours of historical research which laid the groundwork for this volume. Also thanks to Richard Bartlett for his aid during the initial conceptualization of this book.

Finally, special thanks to Hoag Levins, whose writing and organizational abilities brought this project from chaos to completion.

Dedicated
to my warmest friend ever,
Phillip J. Kurtz, Sr.

Preface

This book grew out of the experiences and photographic vision of James A. Warner. Over the last decade, Mr. Warner has avidly sought out and highlighted those pockets of Americana where many of the old traditions, as well as the old songs, have been preserved. The photo compositions on these pages are vivid proof that the people and the places of the good old days have not vanished completely but have just become harder to find.

The songs which the author has chosen to accompany his illustrations constitute a brief musical history of our country during all the various plateaus of its development. In spirit, as well as in musical image, they take us from the tea-dumping days in Boston, through the great push West, to the successes and failures of those learning to live on the vast land they had conquered.

Most of these songs were written anonymously and passed on to us from mouth to mouth. Many were originally composed as the musical accompaniment to a pickaxe, or marching boots, or the clank of shovels in the raw earth. Only later were the songs formalized with banjoes or guitars, and it is the very rawness of their source which gives these songs such power. They are the story of a million biceps in the cotton fields, the tales of barrels of sweat and prisons full of screams. They are the tunes of conquered mountains and killer rivers and bones crumbling in the sun. These are the songs of courage and cowardice and a hundred different battles.

With all their tragedies and triumphs, these are the songs which made America.

Hoag Levins
1972

Contents

Songs That Made America

Yankee Doodle

Fa - th'r and I went down to camp, A -

long with Cap - tain Good - in', And

there we saw the men and boys As

thick as hast - y pud - din'.

Chorus

Yan - kee Doo - dle keep. it up,

Yan - kee Doo - dle dan - dy

Mind the mu - sic and the step And

with the girls be hand - y.

Yankee Doodle went to town,
Riding on a pony,
Stuck a feather in his hat
And called it macaroni.

Chorus:

Yankee doodle, doodle doo,
Yankee doodle dandy,
All the lads and lassies are
Sweet as sugar candy.

Additional British verses:

And there they'd fife away like fun,
And play on cornstalk fiddles,
And some had ribbons red as blood
All bound about their middles.

Uncle Sam came there to change
Some pancakes and some onions
For lassies' cake to carry home
To give his wife and young ones.

Cornwallis's Country Dance

The American troops put together still another set of lyrics:

Cornwallis led a country dance,
The like was never seen, sir!
Much retrograde and much advance
And all with General Greene, sir!

Greene, in the South, then danced a set,
And got a mighty name, sir!
Cornwallis jigged with young 'Fayette
But suffered in his fame, sir!

Quoth he, "My guards are weary grown
With footing country dances;
They never at St. James's shone
At capers, kicks, or prances."

His music soon forgets to play,
His feet no more can move, sir!

And all his bands now curse the day
They jigged to our shores, sir!

Now, Tories all, what can ye say?
Come, this is not a griper:
That while your hopes are danced away
'Tis you must pay the piper.

There is no more logical place for a list of American folk songs to begin than with "Yankee Doodle." This familiar ditty probably goes back as far as one could possibly dig in search of the very beginnings—not only of American folk music but of America itself.

Originally written by anonymous members of the British Redcoats after the Boston Tea Party, the lyrics were meant to taunt and belittle the shabby forces of the Colonial militiamen. The British soldiers, under the command of "Gentleman Johnny" Burgoyne, sang the song as they disembarked in Boston Harbor. Their mission was to put down the upstart Yankee dandies who were rattling sabers and throwing about careless talk of a break from England.

The Yankee doodlers soon proved to be more of an opponent than the British had casually anticipated. At the battles of Bunker Hill, Kings Mountain, Cowpens, Yorktown, and others, the unkempt militiamen of George Washington cut the polished British regulars to ribbons.

Adopting the Redcoat tune as their own victory song, the American soldiers rewrote the lyrics as the sarcastic story of "Cornwallis's Country Dance."

On October 19, 1781, that new, Americanized version of "Yankee Doodle" was played as the final, vengeful touch during the ceremony in which British General Cornwallis officially surrendered.

Ring Around the Rosy

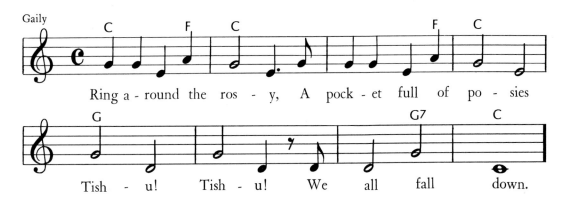

Ring a - round the ros - y, A pock - et full of po - sies

Tish - u! Tish - u! We all fall down.

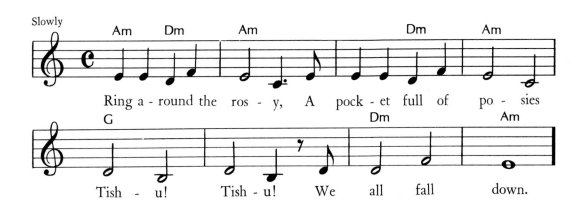

Ring a - round the ros - y, A pock - et full of po - sies

Tish - u! Tish - u! We all fall down.

"Ring Around the Rosy" has come down to us today as one of the most frequently heard children's songs. Originally a native English tune, the chanting singsong is now as common to American kindergarten classes as chalkboards or finger paints.

Historians find this hard to explain, since the verse was first written as a sardonic commentary on the bubonic plague. The words are actually a graphic description of how the disease infects and finally kills its victims.

The song evolved in 1665 as the Black Death of the plague raged across England and, in just a few months, killed one-fifth the population of London.

Plague-stricken victims would first develop purple blotches on their bodies which physicians called "rosies." Because of the phenomenal rate of death, corpses would often lie for days or weeks on the streets of London before being buried. Burial crews, seeking to ward off the nausea caused by the reeking corpses, filled their pockets with aromatic posies and would crush the petals to release even more of the pleasant odors.

Just before the plague victims expired, they suffered fits of sneezing ("tishu!, tishu!") and then would "all fall down," dead.

Steal Away

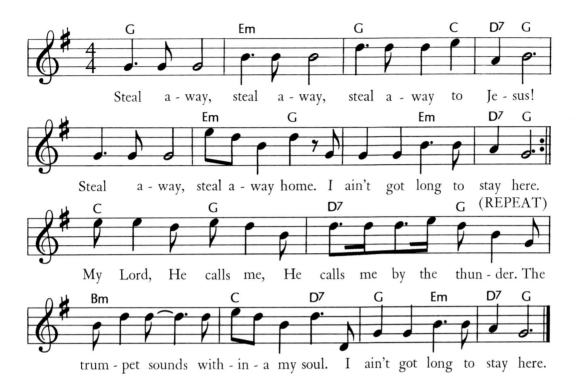

Steal a - way, steal a - way, steal a - way to Je - sus! Steal a - way, steal a - way home. I ain't got long to stay here. My Lord, He calls me, He calls me by the thun - der. The trum - pet sounds with - in - a my soul. I ain't got long to stay here.

Green trees a-bendin'
Poor sinner stands a-tremblin'
The trumpet sounds within-a my soul.
I ain't got long to stay here.

Songs such as this one were commonplace in the everyday life of black plantation slaves. Much more than a work song, this tune is actually a coded message which could be sung across the fields without attracting the critical attention of the white overlords.

Many Southern plantation owners, afraid of anything which provided some cohesive thread of unity among their slaves, forbade blacks to practice the religion which white missionaries had taught them in the early years of slavery. Religion, therefore, became highly clandestine; news of secret prayer meetings or related events could be passed on only in ways which escaped the whites.

Songs like "Steal Away" were sung by a black preacher and then picked up and passed on across the acres of cotton. In this particular version, word is being passed to "steal away"—not to Jesus as the lyrics say but rather to a secret meeting place. In this case, the slaves met at a large willow tree in the swamp ("Green trees a-bendin' ").

"Steal Away" is known to have been written by Aba Ouigi, a slave preacher whose name was changed to Charles by his white owner. Ouigi rose to a position of great power among Georgia slaves and enjoyed a large religious following. Like so many other blacks, however, he was discovered leading a secret prayer meeting and killed by white men who kicked him to death.

All the Pretty Little Horses

Hush - you - bye, Don't you cry, Go to sleep - y lit - tle ba - by.

When you wake, you shall have All the pret - ty lit - tle hor - ses.

Blacks and bays, Dap - ples and grays, Coach and six - a lit - tle hor - ses.

Hush - you - bye, Don't you cry, Go to sleep - y lit - tle ba - by.

Hush-you-bye,
Don't you cry,
Go to sleepy, little baby.
Way down yonder,
In de medder,
Lies a po' lil' lambie.
De bees an' de butterflies
Peckin' out his eyes,
De po' lil' thing cried, "Mammy!"
Hush-you-bye,
Don't you cry,
Go to sleepy, little baby.

This lilting and familiar lullaby first evolved in the early 1800's. For years it was a standard among black women humming their children to sleep or calming the young ones in times of distress.

Legend has it that the song was widely popularized after a wandering singer added words to the tune and brought it North. The story goes that a vagabond singer, who had stopped to rest at the home of a black sharecropper, heard the man's wife singing her daughter to sleep. Caught up in the gentle melody, the singer promised to put words

to it. As he was gazing out at the horizon, he saw a herd of horses being driven by. They provided him with the necessary inspiration, and we were given a lovely, soothing song to go to sleep by.

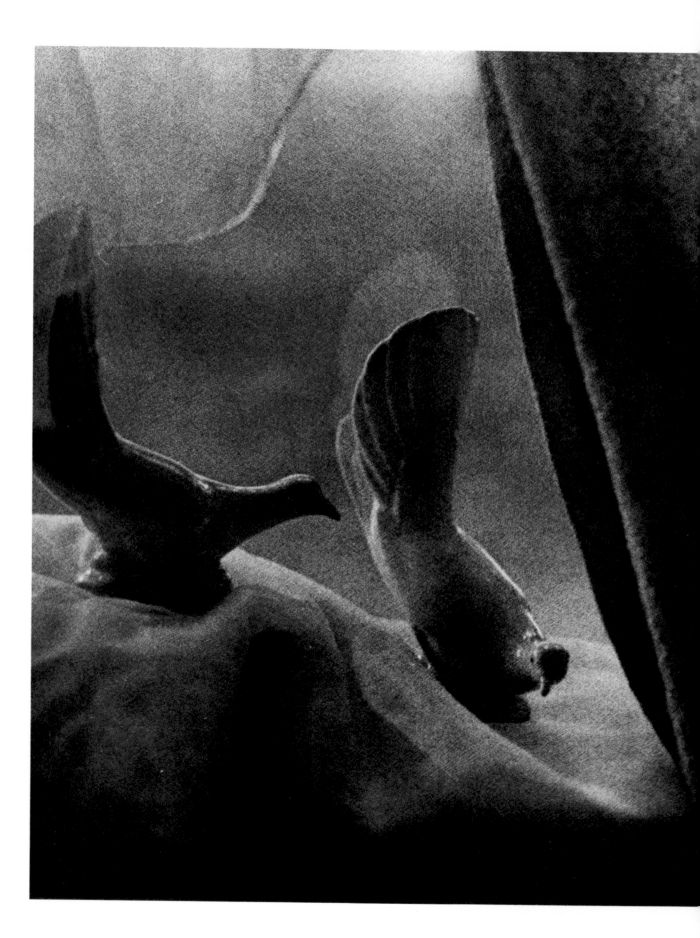

Turtle Dove

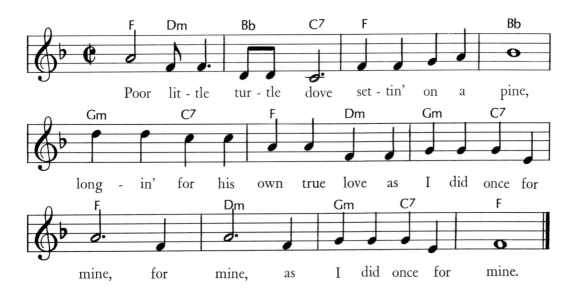

Poor lit-tle tur-tle dove set-tin' on a pine, long-in' for his own true love as I did once for mine, for mine, as I did once for mine.

> I come down from the mountain side
> I give my horn a blow
> Every one of those pretty little gals
> Said, "Yonder goes my beau, my beau!
> Yonder goes my beau!"
>
> I went down to the valley green
> To win to me my love
> When I got done with that pretty little gal
> She turned to a turtle dove, a dove,
> She turned to a turtle dove.
>
> I walked down the street that very same night
> In my heart was a sweet, sweet song
> But I got in a fight and in jail all night
> And every durned thing went wrong, went wrong,
> Every durned thing went wrong.
>
> *(Repeat verse one)*

The turtle dove has often turned up as a dominant theme in American folklore. Taken as the sign of peace and hope, and frequently mentioned in the Bible, the bird has been celebrated in countless songs.

In this particular song, the creature is the focal point of a simple story which pleases the ear and captures a bit of the earthiness of the frontier mountain life in Tennessee.

De Boll Weevil

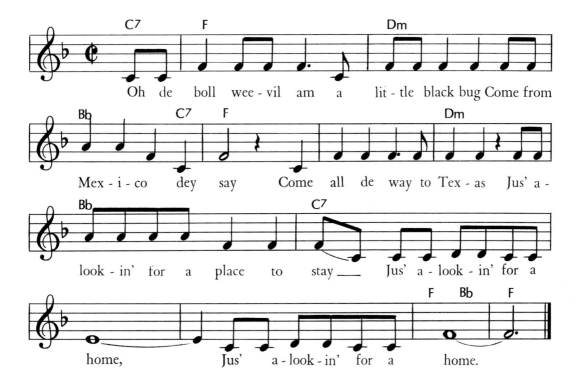

Oh de boll wee-vil am a lit-tle black bug Come from Mex-i-co dey say Come all de way to Tex-as Jus' a-look-in' for a place to stay ___ Jus' a-look-in' for a home, Jus' a-look-in' for a home.

De first time I seen de boll weevil
He was settin' on de square.
De nex' time I seen de boll weevil
He had his whole damn family there
Jus' lookin' for a home, jus' lookin' for a home.

De farmer say to de weevil,
"What makes your head so red?"
De weevil say to de farmer,
"It's a wonder I ain' dead!
Ah lookin' for a home, jus' lookin' for a home."

De farmer take de boll weevil
An' he put him in de hot san'.
De weevil say, "Dis is mighty hot
But I'll stand it like a man!
Dis'll be my home, it'll be my home."

De farmer take de boll weevil
An' he put him in a lump of ice.
De boll weevil say to de farmer,

"Dis is mighty cool an' nice!
It'll be my home, dis'll be my home."

De farmer take de boll weevil
An' he put him in de fire.
De boll weevil say to de farmer,
"Here I are! Here I are!
Dis'll be my home, it'll be my home."

De boll weevil say to de farmer,
"You better leave me alone!
I done et all your cotton,
Now I'm gonna start on your corn!
I'll have a home, I'll have a home!"

De merchant got half de cotton
De boll weevil got de res'.
Didn't leave de farmer's wife
But one ol' cotton dress
An' it's full of holes, it's full of holes!

De farmer say to de merchant,
"We's in an awful fix!
De boll weevil et all de cotton
Up an' lef us only sticks!
We got no home, we got no home!"

De farmer say to de merchant,
"We ain't made but only one bale
An' befoh we'll give you dat one
We'll fight an' go to jail!
We'll have a home, we'll have a home!"

De cap'n say to de missus,
"Now what do you think of that?
De boll weevil done make a nest
In my best Sunday hat!
Goin' to have a home, goin' to have a home!"

Now if anybody should ask you
Who it was dat make dis song
Just say that it was a big black man
Wid a pair of blue duckins on
He ain' got no home, ain' got no home!

This song was written by a black sharecropper who, along with thousands of others in the late 1800's, lost his home and possessions to the boll weevil. Underneath their wry humor, the lyrics capture much of the bitter frustration caused by the swarms of cotton-eating beetles which migrated into American fields from Mexico in 1892.

Attacking the "squares"—as the buds of the cotton plants are called—the weevils devoured the silky seed pod fibers and deposited a load of eggs. One of the biggest little problems ever to threaten the country's farmers, the insects not only had a voracious appetite but could produce as many as five new generations of offspring per season.

By the billions, the bugs ate their way across the vast Southern cotton belts, crippling much of the nation's agriculturally based economy.

Nearly as hardy as they were hungry, the weevils thwarted all the farmers' desperate attempts to find an effective form of control. They were sprayed, picked, iced, burned, squashed, powdered . . . and still they ate on, "lookin' for a home."

It wasn't until well into the 1900's that weevil-killing pesticides such as calcium arsenate were developed, and the notorious insect passed on—out of the cotton fields and into the pages of folklore.

Black Is the Color

Slowly

Black, black, black is the col - or of my true love's hair. Her

lips _____ are like some ros - y fair The

pret - ti - est face and the neat - est ___ hands, I

love _____ the ground where on she stands.

I love my love and well she knows
I love the grass whereon she goes.
If she on earth no more I see
My life will quickly fade away.

I go to troublesome to mourn and weep
But satisfied I ne'er could sleep.
I'll write to you in a few little lines,
I'll suffer death ten thousand times.

So fare you well, my own true love,
The time has passed and I wish you well.
But still I hope the time will come
When you and I will be as one.

This song, known to have been a favorite among singers of the late 1700's, has gone through a number of mutations in the last two centuries. The title has been changed almost as often as the lyrics, while the tune's actual origin has been lost somewhere in a web of colorful legends.

The tale most frequently accompanying the song, however, is the story of Barton

Fink, an emotionally disturbed cripple who lived in the English village of Sedberg.

Fink's physical handicap kept him from a regular job in the local factories, but he was often retained as an errand boy by factory bosses. Despised for his easy job by fellow workers, the boy was blamed whenever one of the workers was caught stealing. Workers claimed they had been informed, or "finked," on.

Fink is said to have fallen in love with the most beautiful girl in the village. Worshipping her from a distance, he was never able to muster the courage to meet her face to face. Hobbling after her on his twisted legs, the youth idolized the girl in poems and songs.

Angered by the ogling cripple who constantly trailed his sister, the girl's brother eventually beat Fink to death.

The raven-haired girl is then said to have found a piece of paper in the dead cripple's hand. On it were written the words of "Black Is the Color." She put the verse to a tune on her mandolin and passed it on to other singers.

I'm Gonna Leave Old Texas Now!

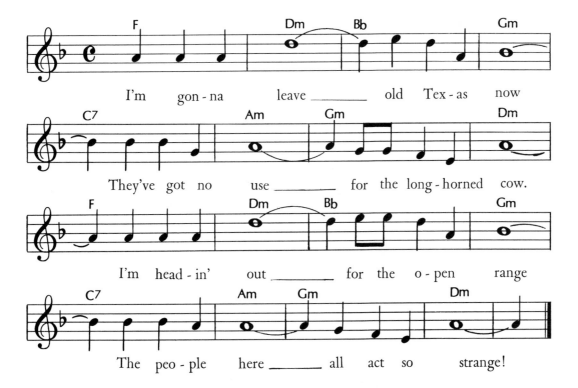

I'm gon-na leave _____ old Tex-as now

They've got no use _____ for the long-horned cow.

I'm head-in' out _____ for the o-pen range

The peo-ple here _____ all act so strange!

Sayin' *adios* to the Alamo
And hit the trail for Mexico
Where the wide, wide earth will be my bed
On my saddle seat I'll rest my head.

When my time on earth is done
I'll take my turn with the Holy One!
I'll tell Saint Peter that I know
A cowboy's soul ain't white as snow.

But way out on the prairie land
He sometimes acted like a man!

The people this song accuses of being "so strange" and having "no use for the long-horned cow" were the small farmers who poured into the Southwestern states in the 1870's. The region's cowboys, accustomed to unrestricted grazing rights for their steers, had little patience with the new settlers who fenced them in with barbed wire and acres of crops.

More than a few times, animosities between the two groups flared into bloody range wars, clandestine wire-cutting campaigns, or herd stampeding. In spite of all this, the

flow of farmers increased; barbed wire salesmen had a field day; and the corn grew fat and high. The need for able cowboys quickly declined.

Many of the die-hard cowpunchers—such as the song's author—abandoned Texas and headed for Mexico, where they enjoyed a few more years of the good old days before the fence stringers and corn growers caught up with them.

Erie Canal

We were for-ty miles from Al-ba-ny, For-get it I nev-er shall. What a ter-ri-ble storm we had one night on the E-ri-e Ca-nal!

Chorus

The E-ri-e was a-ris-in', the gin was a-git-tin' low, And I scarce-ly think we'll git a drink till we git to Buf-fa-lo, _____ till we git to Buf-fa-lo.

The captain he come up on deck,
With a spyglass in his hand.
The fog it was so tarnal thick
He couldn't spy the land.

(Chorus)

Our cook she was a grand old gal,
She wore a ragged dress.
We hoisted her upon a pole
As a signal of distress.

(Chorus)

The captain he got married,
The cook she went to jail.

And I'm the only son-of-a-gun
That's left to tell the tale.

(Chorus)

The barge captain in this song who found himself in such a fog that he couldn't spy the land was in one hell of a fog. The Erie Canal was hardly wider than an oversized drainage ditch, and the barges were always within a few feet of the Canal's earthen banks.

But then, bargemen were well known as braggards and spinners of highly exaggerated tales. The daily life on the Canal was not nearly as glamorous as song writers such as this one would have us believe.

Opened in 1825, the 360-mile, man-made waterway linked Albany on the Hudson River with Buffalo on Lake Erie. The Canal spurred a new era of industrial expansion as the factories of the eastern New York area were afforded easy access to the Great Lakes region. Millions of tons of raw material and finished goods traveled up and down the Canal on clumsy barges which were propelled by bargemen poling the shallow bottom or pulled by mules on the shore.

To the chagrin of many deep-water sailors, the bargemen liked to think of themselves as seafaring men. The question of who was or wasn't a real "sailor" was the cause of more than a few bar brawls in Buffalo and Albany.

Priding themselves on the amount of liquor they could hold, the storms they could brave, and the fighters they could lick, the bargemen sang on, accompanying themselves with banjoes, mouth organs, and well-oiled imaginations.

Wayfarin' Stranger

41

I know dark clouds will gather 'round me,
I know my way is steep and rough,
But beauteous fields lie just beyond me
Where souls redeemed their vigil keep.
I'm goin' there to meet my mother,
She said she'd meet me when I come,
I'm only goin' over Jordan,
I'm only goin' over home.

I want to wear a crown of glory
When I get home to that bright land.
I want to shout salvation's story
In concert with that blood-washed band.
I'm goin' there to meet my Saviour!
To sing His praises evermore!
I'm only goin' over Jordan,
I'm only goin' over home.

This is one of the many lively songs which have come to us as a direct result of the various religious movements which have rippled across the country through the years.

By the 1800's, Americans had taken their parents' old European religious customs and shaken much of the stiffness out of them. The severe, puritanical traditions were substantially loosened and embellished to give us such things as the bench-rocking, foot-stomping, purely American "camp meetings."

Throughout the country, and particularly in the South, camp preachers drew crowds of thousands to their countryside retreats. There, for days on end, there would be singing, wailing, repenting, and other forms of highly vocal tributes to the Almighty.

One of the major features of the camps was the "mourners' bench." There, a person so moved could recite his sins publicly and request forgiveness of God as well as of his tambourine-tapping compatriots. The bench soon became a ministage of sorts, and the confessions often took on the air of small production numbers, complete with songs, screams, and other forms of personal showmanship.

"Wayfarin' Stranger" was born on the "bench," crooned spontaneously in 1801 by a Kentucky mountaineer who is said to have hunted much better than he sang.

Taps

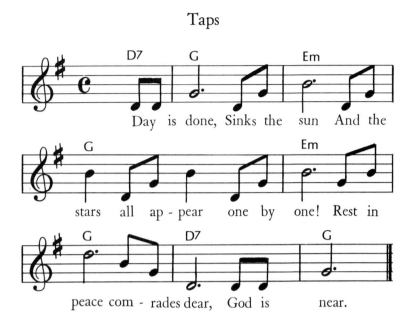

Day is done, Sinks the sun And the stars all ap-pear one by one! Rest in peace com-rades dear, God is near.

Strangely enough, this song, which is so strongly connected to our thoughts of death and burial, was actually composed specifically to save lives.

Early in June of 1862, Union and Confederate armies maneuvered about the country-side of Virginia for weeks, regrouping and seeking favorable positions against each other. Finally, on June 25, they came together on the peninsula at Seven Pines in what was to become known as the Seven Days Battle.

The running battle resulted in forty-three thousand casualties, and bodies were strewn for miles across the densely wooded land.

Forced by the terrain to camp within shooting range of the tattered Confederate forces, Union soldiers, under General Daniel Butterfield, attempted to bury their dead. The burial ceremonies were repeatedly interrupted by Confederate soldiers firing on the graveyard details. Each time the Union soldiers fired a ceremonial volley above the fresh graves, the Confederates, thinking they were again under attack, returned the fire.

Determined that his dead would be buried with the proper ceremony, Butterfield himself sat down and composed a short tune for his bugler. He called the song "Taps" and ordered it played over the graves in the place of the normal rifle volleys. The haunting song saved the lives of many Union army burial team members, and it soon caught on as a ceremonial song throughout the Union army.

Hal-Le-Lu

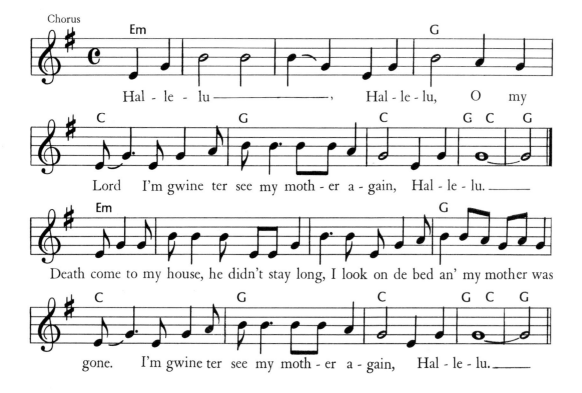

Chorus

Hal - le - lu ————————, Hal - le - lu, O my Lord I'm gwine ter see my moth - er a - gain, Hal - le - lu. ————

Death come to my house, he didn't stay long, I look on de bed an' my mother was gone. I'm gwine ter see my moth - er a - gain, Hal - le - lu. ————

Death come to my house, he didn't stay long,
I look on de bed an' my father was gone.
I'm gwine ter see my father again, etc.

Death come to my house, he didn't stay long,
I look on de bed an' my sister was gone.
I'm gwine ter see my sister again, etc.

Death come to my house, he didn't stay long,
I look on de bed an' my brother was gone.
I'm gwine ter see my brother again, etc.

This black spiritual has been sung at prayer meetings and funerals for at least the last hundred years. The precise circumstances surrounding its origin are not known, but its lyrics lay down a story line which is not hard to identify with, no matter what our background.

Grey Goose

Last Sun - day morn - in', Lord, Lord, Lord!

Last Sun - day morn - in', Lord, Lord, Lord!

Man went a-huntin'
Lord, Lord, Lord!
Man went a-huntin'
Lord, Lord, Lord!

He went huntin' for the grey goose,
He went huntin' for the grey goose.

An' he took along his shotgun,
Yes, he took along his shotgun.

An' along came a grey goose,
Yes, along came a grey goose.

Well, it was up to his shoulder,
An' he pulled back the hammer.

An' the gun went baloom-boom,
Yes, the gun went baloom-boom.

He was six weeks a-fallin',
He was six weeks a-fallin'.

An' they had a feather-pickin',
Yes, they had a feather-pickin'.

He was one year a-cookin',
He was one year a-cookin'.

Then they put him on the table,
Yes, they put him on the table.

The knife couldn't cut him,
No, the knife couldn't cut him.

The fork couldn't stick him,
No, the fork couldn't stick him.

And the saw couldn't cut him,
He broke the saw's tooth out.

An' the last time I seen him,
Oh, the last time I seen him.

He was flyin' over the ocean,
He was flyin' over the ocean.

With a long string of goslin's,
With a long string of goslin's.

Another of the countless songs which grew out of the black slave experience, this seemingly innocuous song about the grey goose is actually a boast of black resistance.

Unable to sing or speak openly of their feelings, the blacks were forced to express their sentiments cached behind harmless symbolism in their song lyrics. Sung lustily in the presence of whites, this song conveyed a deep feeling of secret community among the slave singers.

The grey goose of the lyrics is a symbolic representation of the inner spirit of the black field laborers. Forced to live with the reality of their enslaved bodies, they liked to boast in such songs as this one that there was at least some part of each of them which could neither be cut, nor sawed, nor threatened with a shotgun.

Pick a Bale of Cotton

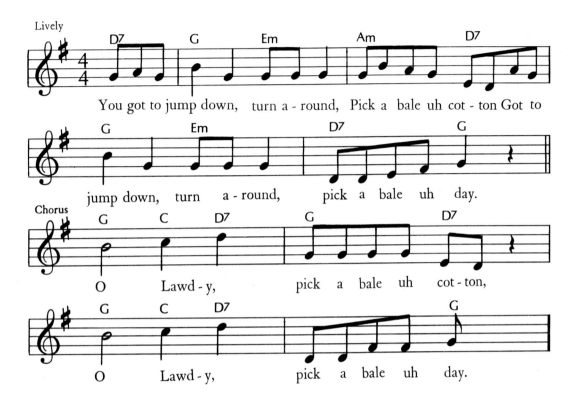

Lively

D7   G   Em   Am   D7

You got to jump down, turn a-round, Pick a bale uh cot-ton Got to

G   Em   D7   G

jump down, turn a-round, pick a bale uh day.

Chorus

G   C   D7   G   D7

O   Lawd-y,   pick a bale uh cot-ton,

G   C   D7   G

O   Lawd-y,   pick a bale uh day.

Me an' muh podner can
Pick a bale uh cotton
Me an' muh podner can
Pick a bale uh day.

(Chorus)

Me an' muh wife can
Pick a bale uh cotton
Me an' muh wife can
Pick a bale uh day.

(Chorus)

Had a little woman could
Pick a bale uh cotton,
Had a little woman could
Pick a bale uh day.

(Chorus)

The monotony of cotton picking has fathered scores of songs throughout the years. "Pick a Bale of Cotton" has survived as perhaps the most memorable of the plantation field working songs.

Popularized in the early 1900's by black folk singer Huddie (Leadbelly) Ledbetter, the song was originally sung by field hands trying to pass the time, as well as forget the pains in their fingers.

Extracting the delicate fibers from the thorny pod of the cotton plant was tedious work which became the center of many tall tales. Braggards liked to insist that they could pick more cotton than anyone else. Their imaginations often prompted them to claim they could even "pick a bale uh day."

In reality, picking a full bale of cotton in a single day was an impossible feat, even for five seasoned workers, let alone only one.

Shenandoah[1]

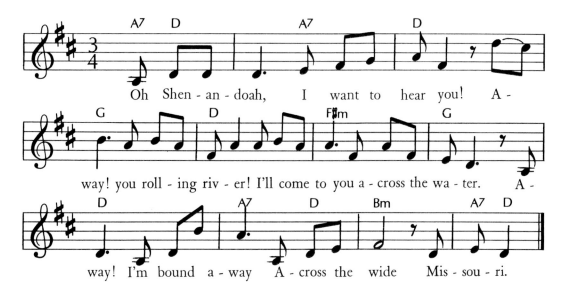

Oh Shen - an - doah, I want to hear you! A-
way! you roll - ing riv - er! I'll come to you a - cross the wa - ter. A-
way! I'm bound a - way A - cross the wide Mis - sou - ri.

The old Missouri's a mighty river.
Away! you rolling river!
The Indians camp along her border.
Away! We're bound away
Across the wide Missouri.

A young man loved an Indian maiden.
Away! you rolling river!
And his canoe with gifts was laden.
Away! We're bound away
Across the wide Missouri.

Oh Shenandoah! I'll never leave you.
Away! you rolling river!
Shenandoah, I'll never grieve you.
Away! I'm bound away
Across the wide Missouri.

The geographical splendor of the Shenandoah Valley inspired dozens of stories, legends, and songs among the Americans who initially settled in the area along the Missouri. Down through the years, the word "Shenandoah" took on an almost mythical meaning for all those who had heard of, but never visited, the region. Many exaggerated stories were circulated describing the great valley where Indians were friendly, game was plentiful, and crops grew higher and healthier than anywhere else.

[1] Although notation is important in any song, in this case it is a guideline only, for many parts of the song, as in *Away!,* may be held as long as the singer desires.

This particular Shenandoah song became a favorite line-hauling chanty among American seamen, who are said to have sung its gentle lyrics to calm their pangs of homesickness and melancholia.

The Battle Hymn of the Republic

Mine eyes have seen the glo - ry of the com - ing of the Lord. He is tram - pling out the vin - tage where the grapes of wrath are stored. He has loosed the fate - ful light - ning of his ter - ri - ble swift sword. His truth is march - ing on.

Chorus

Glo - ry, glo - ry, Hal - le - lu - jah! Glo - ry, glo - ry, Hal - le - lu - jah! Glo - ry, glo - ry, Hal - le - lu - jah! His truth is march - ing on!

John Brown's Body

John Brown's body lies a-moldrin' in his grave
John Brown's body lies a-moldrin' in his grave
John Brown's body lies a-moldrin' in his grave
But his soul goes marching on, etc.

Steffe's Song

Brother, will you meet me by Canaan's happy shore?

(Repeat twice)

To watch the Jordan roll.

Standard practice among folk singers has always been to take any good song, bend and stretch it a little according to fancy, and then sing the reworked song as their own. Most of the folk songs we know today have come a long way from where they originally started. Each song in this book has its own such story of evolution, but probably none is quite as colorful as that of "The Battle Hymn of the Republic."

At the height of his career as a Bible Belt preacher in 1853, William Steffe wrote a song to accompany his sermons at camp meetings. The Charleston, South Carolina, black man penned a tune called "Brother, Will You Meet Me by Canaan's Happy Shore?".

So catchy and memorable was Steffe's heaven-praising ditty that it was soon being hummed far and wide. It swiftly became a favorite around the campfires of the drifters, hobos, and roustabouts wandering through the region.

One of these drifters, Thomas Bishop, of Vermont, took the tune with him as he traveled north through South Carolina toward Boston, where he joined the Union army as an infantryman.

Bishop was a member of the division which helped thwart John Brown's famed raid on Harper's Ferry. He immortalized the raid in lyrics set to Steffe's tune, which became widely known as "John Brown's Body."

This "new" tune quickly spread through the ranks of Yankee soldiers, where it was once again altered by enthusiastic amateur lyricists. The soldiers took the once evangelical song and made it an endless string of verses about the bawdy women, easy liquor, and bar brawls which spiced their lives and dreams.

So it went until 1861, when Julia Ward Howe, appalled by the unspeakably obscene marching song being sung by the Union troops passing her Washington, D.C., home, penned a new version. This one retained much of the religious flavor intended by the song's creator and began with the now familiar words, "Mine eyes have seen the glory of the coming of the Lord."

The Streets of Laredo

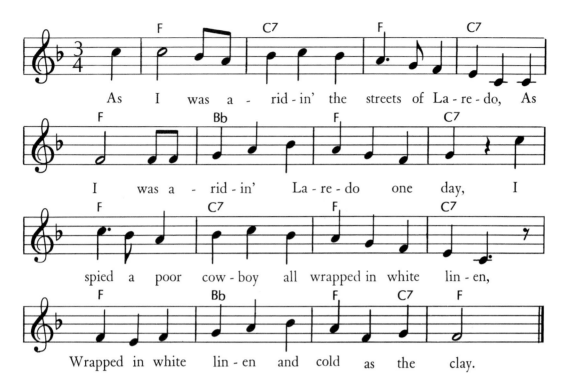

As I was a - rid - in' the streets of La - re - do, As
I was a - rid - in' La - re - do one day, I
spied a poor cow - boy all wrapped in white lin - en,
Wrapped in white lin - en and cold as the clay.

"I see by your outfit that you are a cowboy."
These words he did say as I slowly rode by.
"Come dismount beside me and hear my sad story,
I'm shot in the breast and I know I must die."

"Once in the saddle I used to go dashing,
Once in the saddle I used to go gay,
First down to Rosie's and then to the cardhouse,
Now I'm shot in the breast and I'm dyin' today."

"Beat the drum slowly and play the fife lowly,
Play the dead march as they carry me along,
Take me to the green valley there to lay the sod o'er me,
I'm a poor lonesome cowboy and I know I've done wrong."

"Get six jolly cowboys to carry my coffin,
Six pretty maidens to bear up my pall,
Throw bunches of roses all over my casket,
Roses to deaden the clods as they fall."

"Please bring me a cup of cool spring water
To ease my parched lips," the cowboy then said.

But when I came back his poor soul had then left him,
He'd gone to his Maker—the cowboy was dead.

We beat the drum slowly and played the fife slowly,
We kept to the dead march as we bore him along,
For he was our comrade, so brave and so daring
That handsome young cowboy who knew he'd done wrong.

This lyrical lament for the dying victim of a shoot-out on the streets of Laredo, Texas, has changed substantially since it was first written in 1711 as the story of an Irish soldier infected with venereal disease.

Initially penned as an Irish funeral dirge, it was titled "Case of the Unfortunate Rake." That version told the tale of a devil-may-care Irishman stationed with the British army in Northern India. The soldier became involved with a beautiful girl, but eventually died, a victim of the venereal disease she had passed on to him.

The sad plaint became a favorite Irish folk song and, as such, was brought to America in the 1800's by Irish immigrants. It was lyrically updated by an anonymous Irishman who, like many of his fellow immigrants, settled in wild Western towns like Laredo.

Although the story line was changed, the Irish cowboy kept much of the imagery of his homeland in his rewritten version. There were, of course, no fifes and drums to be found in the Old West, just as the practice of wrapping corpses in linen was much more commonly found in Dublin than in places like Laredo.

The Sow Took the Measles

How do you think I be-gan in the world? I got me a sow and sev-'ral oth-er things. The sow took the mea-sles and she died in the spring.

What do you think I made of her hide? The ve-ry best sad-dle that you ev-er did ride! Sad-dle or bri-dle or an-y such thing, The sow took the mea-sles and she died in the spring.

What do you think I made of her hide?
The very best sad-dle that you ev-er did ride!
Sad-dle or bri-dle or an-y such thing,
The sow took the mea-sles and she died in the spring.

What do you think I made of her nose?
The very best thimble that ever sewed clothes!

Thimble or thread or any such thing,
The sow took the measles and she died in the spring.

What do you think I made of her tail?
The very best whup that ever sought sail!
Whup or whup socket or any such thing,
The sow took the measles and she died in the spring.

What do you think I made of her feet?
The very best pickles that you ever did eat!
Pickles or glue or any such thing,
The sow took the measles and she died in the spring.

Just below the surface of the foot-tapping lightness of this song is a very serious story about the rigors of frontier survival.

Often traveling West with no more than an axe, a rifle, and an animal or two, frontier settlers wasted very little—of anything. In such isolated wilderness outposts as Boonesborough and Harrodsburg, Kentucky, it often took as long as six months to a year for ordered supplies to arrive from the East. One learned out of necessity to make do with the materials at hand. It was a severe but nevertheless creative existence, where a bit of work and ingenuity could turn an event like the death of a prized sow into a blessing of sorts.

Hide from the dead animal was worked into leather, while items as the animal's nose and tail were turned into such usable utensils as thimbles and whips.

And even when the animal and all its parts were finally gone, the really creative frontiersman would go still further. He would take the whole event, add some music to it, and hand-craft a pleasant bit of folklore which could be kept next to his fireplace for enjoyment on quiet nights.

The Tenderfoot

One spring - time I thought just fer fun, I'd see how punch - in' cows was done. So when the round - up had be - gun, I went to the cat - tle king. Says he, "My fore - man's gone to town, He's in the sa - loon and his name is Brown. If you see him he'll take you on." Says I, "That's just the thing."

They took me to the ranch next day
Brown augured me 'most all the way
He said, "Cowpunchin's nothin' but play
And there ain't no work at all!
It's only driftin' with the tide
And all you got to do is ride!"
That son of a gun! How he lied!
Don't you think he had his gall?

They put me in charge of the "cavvy" yard
And they told me not to work too hard.
For all I had to do was guard
Them horses from gettin' away.
Though sometimes one would make a break
And across the prairie he would take
Just like he was runnin' for a stake,
To them it seemed like play.

But they had 160 head
And I sometimes wished that I was dead.
When one got away Brown's head turned red
And there was the devil to pay.
Sometimes they'd stumble and then fall,
Sometimes you couldn't head them off at all.
I'd shoot out like a cannonball
Till the ground got in my way.

They put me on board an old gray hack
With two "set-fasts" upon his back.
They bundled him up like a gunny sack,
They used my bed and all.
When I got on he quit the ground
He went up in the air and danced around.
When I come down I busted the ground
And I got one hell of a fall.

They picked me up and they carried me in
And they rubbed me down with an old stake pin.
"That's the way they all begin
And you're doin' swell," says Brown.
"In the mornin', if you don't die,
I'll give you another horse to try."
"Oh say kain't I walk?" says I.
Says Brown, "Yes, back to town."

I've traveled up and I've traveled down,
I've traveled this country all around.
I've lived in the city, I've lived in the town
And I've got this much to say:
Before you try cowpunchin', kiss your wife,
Take a heavy insurance on your life,
Then cut your throat with a Bowie knife.
It's easier done that way!

It has never been easy to be a young newcomer in any field, and cowpunching in the early West was no different. There was a lot to be learned, and no time to learn it before the job began.

This song is a good-natured but woefully told story of one such tenderfoot cowboy assigned to the "cavvy" yard. The yard held the constantly milling herd of cow ponies which was taken along on every cattle drive. In real-life cattle herding (as opposed to the highly glamorized TV and movie variety), cowboys used as many as three and four horses a day while herding. The work was rugged and the animals tired and lost their edge quickly. Every few hours, each cowboy would change his horse for a fresh mount.

The range horses used for cowpunching were a disagreeable lot. Compact, explosive animals, not far removed from the wild, they were rounded up, saddled, and handled with the maximum of caution and physical effort. Highly spirited, they were forever trying to run free; often half a dozen at once would scatter from the cavvy in different directions.

Two men at a time were assigned to cavvy yard duty and there were never any volunteers. The job was dirty, frustrating, and, more often than not, entrusted to the novice cowhands who didn't yet know enough to refuse it.

Lolly-Too-Dum-Day

As I went out one mornin' to take the pleasant
air, Lol-ly- too - dum, too - dum, lol-ly-too-dum-day. As
I went out one morn - in' to take the pleas - ant air, I
o - ver- heard a moth - er a - scold - in' her daugh - ter fair. Lol - ly-
too - dum, too - dum, lol - ly - too - dum - day.

You better go wash them dishes and hush that flatterin' tongue!
Lolly-too-dum, too-dum, lolly-too-dum-day.
You know you want to git married, but gal, you are too young!
Lolly-too-dum, etc.

Oh, pity my condition just like it were your own!
Lolly-too-dum, etc.
For fourteen long years I've been livin' all alone!
Lolly-too-dum, etc.

Supposin' I were willin', where would you git your man?
Lolly-too-dum, etc.
Lawdy, massy, mammy, I'd marry that handsome Sam!
Lolly-too-dum, etc.

Supposin' he should spite you, like you done him before?
Lolly-too-dum, etc.

Lawdy, massy, mammy, I could marry forty more!
Lolly-too-dum, etc.

There's peddlers and there's tinkers and boys from the plow
Lolly-too-dum, etc.
Lawdy, massy, mammy, I'm a-gettin' that feelin' now!
Lolly-too-dum, etc.

Now my daughter's married and well for to do.
Lolly-too-dum, etc.
Gather 'round young fellers, I'm on the market too!
Lolly-too-dum, etc.

This happy-go-lucky song of a frontier man-chaser comes to us from the era of the great Western gold rushes. By the tens of thousands, men gathered in such places as Sutter's Creek, in California, seeking their fortunes with picks and pans.

The male migrations to the gold country were more often than not followed in short order by smaller, but no less determined, waves of shrewd women, many of them accompanied by their daughters.

Even the plainest female face among them had little trouble attracting attention in mining towns where the male-female ratio often ran as high as 200 to 1.

Mothers could sell their daughter's affections to the suitor with the highest bid, and if they were widows—such as the singer of this song—they could double their money by putting themselves "on the market" as well.

The Logger's Boast

Come all ye sons of free - dom through - out the state of Maine, Come all ye gal - lant lum - ber - men and lis - ten to my strain, On the banks of the Pen - ob - scot where the rap - id wa - ters flow,

Chorus

O, we'll range the wild woods o - ver and a - lum - ber - ing we'll go, and a - lum - ber - ing we'll go, O, we'll range the wild woods o - ver while a - lum - ber - ing we'll go.

When the white frost gilds the valleys,
The cold congeals the flood.
When many men have naught to do
To earn their family's bread.
When the swollen streams are frozen
And the hills are clad with snow.

(Refrain)

The music of our burnished axe
Shall make the woods resound.
And many a lofty pine
Will tumble to the ground.

At night, ho! 'round our good campfire
We will sing while rude winds blow.

(Refrain)

When winter's snows are melted
And the icebound streams are free,
We'll run our logs to market
Then haste our friends to see.
How kindly true hearts welcome us
Our wives and children too!

(Refrain)

We will spend with these the summer
And once more a-lumbering we'll go.
We will spend with them the summer
And once more a-lumbering we'll go.

"On the banks of the Penobscot, where the rapid waters flow" was not the safest place for a man to make a living in the late 1700's. More than a few loggers lost their lives to hostile Indians, killer wolves, and temperatures so cold that a cup of hot coffee could freeze solid in the time it took a man to sharpen his axe.

For five months of every year, the logging camps were completely cut off from the outside world. Around them, the woods of Maine were drifted high with tens of feet of snow. The mighty Penobscot itself froze over and became impassable.

Those long, lonely hours of winter were often spent singing songs such as this one, or swapping tales which grew taller between tellings.

Life in the woods was indeed a rugged one, and not many men could muster the physical or mental strength it took to be a logger. But for those that could, there was no other way to live. And there was no song ever sung which was as pretty as the sound of the river ice cracking under the first spring sunshine.

Will You Come to the Bow'r?

Will you come to the bow'r I have shad - ed for you? Our

bed __ shall be ros - es all span - gled with dew. Will you

come to the bow'r I have shad - ed for you? Our

bed ___ shall be ros - es all span - gled with dew.

Will you, will you, will you, will you come to the bow'r?

Will you, will you, will you, will you come to the bow'r?

There under the bow'r on roses you'll lie,
With a blush on your cheek but a smile in your eye.
There under the bow'r on roses you'll lie,
With a blush on your cheek but a smile in your eye.
Will you, will you, will you, will you smile, my beloved?
Will you, will you, will you, will you smile, my beloved?

Legend has it that this is the gentle tune sung on the walls of the Alamo by Davey Crockett shortly before the final charge of Mexican General Santa Anna.

Some thirty noncombatants survived the battle of the Alamo, and one told the story of Crockett's singing. He is said to have repeated the lilting lyrics over and over to calm his own nerves and those of the people around him.

In all probability, the tune was one that the frontiersman had brought with him from his home in Tennessee. It was the last song ever sung by the famed Crockett, or by any of the other 187 Americans defending the Alamo on that day in 1836. After holding off the Mexican army for thirteen days, the fort fell—and every one of its fighting occupants was killed.

Cumberland Gap

Cum - ber - land Gap is a not - ed place,

Three kinds of wa - ter to wash your face.

Cum - ber - land Gap with its cliff and rocks,

Home of the pan - ther, the bear and fox.

The first white man in Cumberland Gap
Was old Doc Walker, an English chap.
Daniel Boone on Pinnacle Rock
Fought off Indians with an old flintlock.

Old Aunt Diana, if you don't keer,
Leave my little jug settin' right here.
If it's not here when I come back,
I'll raise hell in Cumberland Gap.

Old Aunt Diana took a little spell,
Broke my little jug all to hell.
Me and my wife and my wife's grandpap,
We all raised hell in Cumberland Gap.

Here, in short verse, is a brief history of the discovery and development of the Cumberland Gap—America's initial gateway for Westward expansion.

A natural passageway through the rugged Appalachian Mountains, the Gap today marks the spot where the three states of Virginia, Kentucky, and Tennessee meet. In the old days, it provided the first feasible wagon and horse path West through the barrier mountains.

As the song says, the first white man to see the Gap was Doctor Thomas Walker, an Englishman, who, in 1750, set out to find the land known to the Indians as "Kan-ta-ke" or "place of the fields." After a number of unsuccessful attempts to take his party over the mountains, Walker began to search for the great gap which Indian legend said existed.

Some nineteen years after Walker's discovery, the Gap was opened for its first substantial volume of traffic by Daniel Boone, who blazed his famed Wilderness Road.

After the Revolutionary War, thousands of Colonial soldiers, who had been paid with land vouchers instead of money, settled in the Cumberland region. Towns sprung up and the Gap settlements became melting pots of the ideas and people, as well as of the stories and songs, traveling both ways across the country.

Buck-Eye Jim

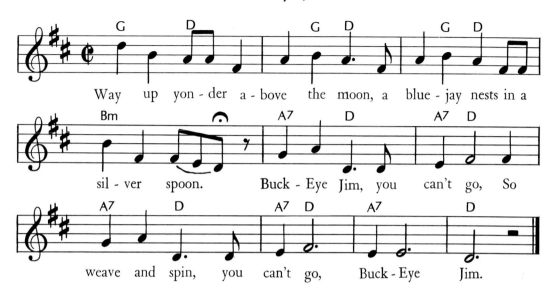

Way up yonder above the moon, a blue-jay nests in a
sil-ver spoon. Buck-Eye Jim, you can't go, So
weave and spin, you can't go, Buck-Eye Jim.

Way up yonder above the sky,
A jaybird built in a bluebird's eye.
Go limber, Jim! You can't go,
So weave and spin, you can't go, Buck-Eye Jim.

Way down yonder by a hollow log,
A red bird danced with a green bullfrog.
Buck-Eye Jim, you can't go,
So weave and spin, you can't go, Buck-Eye Jim.

Way down yonder by a sycamore trough
An old woman died of the whoopin' cough.
Buck-Eye Jim, you can't go,
So weave and spin, you can't go, Buck-Eye Jim.

The early American song writers, drawing from the land around them for imagery in
their lyrics, have given us a virtual zoo of animal-related songs.

This one about blue jays and dancing bullfrogs is among the thousands of odes
written to cattle, horses, dogs, and an infinite variety of birds. Unable to find sympathetic
human ears to which to tell their troubles, countless composers unburdened themselves
to their livestock.

"Buck-Eye Jim" is the lighthearted lament of a young farm boy who would much
rather be anywhere other than at the chores his mother has given him. Unhappy with
the day's task of spinning and weaving, he daydreams about the circus of woodland
animals which calls to him from the open lands beyond his home.

Goober Peas

Sit - ting   by   the   road - side   on   a   sum - mer's   day,

Chat - ting   with   my   mess - mates,   pass - ing   time   a - way,

Ly - ing   in   the   shad - ow   un - der - neath   the   trees,

Good - ness   how   de - li - cious, ___   eat - ing   goo - ber   peas!

Chorus

Peas!   Peas!   Peas!   Peas!   Eat - ing   goo - ber   peas!

Good - ness   how   de - li - cious, ___   eat - ing   goo - ber   peas!

When a horseman passes, the soldiers have a rule
To cry out at their loudest, "Mister, here's your mule!"
But another pleasure enchantinger than these
Is wearing out your grinders, eating goober peas!

(Chorus)

Just before the battle the Gen'ral hears a row.
He says, "The Yanks are coming, I hear their rifles now."
He turns around in wonder, and what do you think he sees?
The Georgia Militia—eating goober peas!

(Chorus)

I think my song has lasted almost long enough,
The subject's interesting, but rhymes are mighty tough.
I wish this war was over, when free from rags and fleas,
We'd kiss our wives and sweethearts and gobble goober peas!

(Chorus)

Composed spontaneously by Confederate soldiers, "Goober Peas" is more than just the silly bit of verse it appears to be at first glance. Written between the lines is a mirthless tale of the final ragtag days of the Southern Confederacy.

In constant flight from the Union armies, with food and ammunition stores gone, and the land around them laid bare by the fires of General Sherman's army, the Grays fended off starvation by foraging goober peas.

Better known as peanuts, only the "peas," growing deep underground, survived the fires which decimated all above-ground crops.

The goobers were eaten morning, noon, and night, washed down with "Confederate coffee"—an acrid drink brewed from parched rye and water.

Take This Hammer

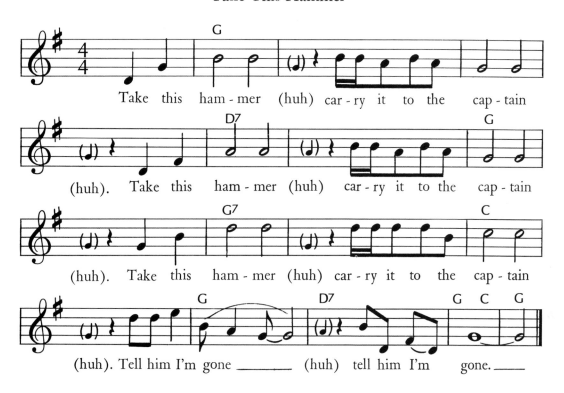

Take this ham-mer (huh) car-ry it to the cap-tain (huh). Take this ham-mer (huh) car-ry it to the cap-tain (huh). Take this ham-mer (huh) car-ry it to the cap-tain (huh). Tell him I'm gone _____ (huh) tell him I'm gone. _____

If he ask you (huh) was I runnin' (huh)

(Repeat twice)

Tell him I was flyin' (huh) tell him I was flyin' (huh).

If he ask you (huh) was I laughin' (huh)

(Repeat twice)

Tell him I was cryin' (huh) tell him I was cryin' (huh).

I don' want no (huh) cold iron shackles (huh)

(Repeat twice)

Roun' my leg (huh) roun' my leg (huh).

I don' want no (huh) peas, pone, or 'lasses (huh)

(Repeat twice)

They hurt my pride (huh) they hurt my pride (huh).

Cap'n call me (huh) a nappy-headed devil (huh)

(Repeat twice)

It ain' my name (huh) it ain' my name (huh).

Cap'n got a big gun (huh) he wanna play it bad (huh)
(*Repeat twice*)
Gonna take it in the mornin' (huh) if'n he make me mad (huh).

Take this hammer (huh) take it to the captain (huh)
(*Repeat twice*)
Tell him I'm gone (huh) tell him I'm gone (huh).

If any one place had to be singled out as the richest source of American folk song material, it might well be the country's prisons. Many of our most renowned folk singers—past and present—have drawn heavily on the harshness and deprivation of a prisoner's life for lyrical material. A great many of these songs—such as this one—are the products of firsthand experience on chain gangs or behind the walls.

"Take This Hammer" was sung loud and often by the prison chain gangs who built vast stretches of road through the postwar South.

Emphatically Negroid in its essential flavor and wording, the song says much about the condition of prison laborers in the period immediately following the Civil War. Many states, including most Southern ones, became notorious for their inhuman treatment of prisoners, particularly black ones. At a time when blacks comprised less than one-third of the total population of the South, they made up almost 90 percent of every Southern prison role. It was often charged that the only crime many of these blacks had committed was the unfortunate one of living in a state that needed roads built.

Kept on the job for twelve and fifteen hours a day and fed only rough corn pone, dried cowpeas, and sorghum molasses, the prisoners worked out their long stretches on the business end of hammers, picks, and shovels.

Helping to pass the time with the familiar songs of their farm and plantation lives, the black laborers also amalgamated their prison experiences into their personal song books. Forbidden to speak to the captain of the work crew for any reason, prisoners often cursed and taunted "the man" in the lyrics of their work songs.

The Lane County Bachelor

My __ name is Frank Bo-lar, 'nole bach-'lor I am, __ I'm
My __ house it is built of the na-tion-al soil, __ The

keep-ing-ing old bach on an el-e-gant plan. __ You'll
walls are e-rec-ted ac-cord-ing to Hoyle. __ The

find me out West in the coun-ty of Lane
roof has no pitch but is lev-el and plain And I

Starv-ing to death on a gov-ern-ment claim.
al-ways get wet when it hap-pens to rain.

Chorus

But hur-rah for Lane Coun-ty, the land of the free, __ The

home of the grass-hop-per, bed-bug and flea. __ I'll

sing loud her prais-es and boast of her fame, While

starv-ing to death on my gov-ern-ment claim.

But hur - rah for Lane Coun - ty, the land of the free,
The home of the grass - hop - per, bed - bug and flea.
I'll sing loud her prais - es and boast of her fame,
While starv - ing to death on my gov - ern - ment claim.

My clothes, they are ragged, my language is rough,
My head is case-hardened, both solid and tough.
The dough it is scattered all over the room,
And the floor would get scared at the sight of a broom.
My dishes are dirty and some in the bed,
Covered with sorghum and government bread.
But I have a good time, and live at my ease
On common sop sorghum, old bacon, and grease.

But hurrah for Lane County, the land of the West,
Where the farmers and laborers are always at rest.
Where you've nothing to do but sweetly remain,
And starve like a man on your government claim.

How happy I am when I crawl into bed,
And a rattlesnake rattles his tail at my head.
And the gay little centipede, void of all fear,
Crawls over my pillow and into my ear.
And the nice little bedbug so cheerful and bright
Keeps me a-scratching full half of the night.
And the gay little flea with toes sharp as a tack,
Plays, "Why don't you catch me?" all over my back.

But hurrah for Lane County, where blizzards arise,
Where the winds never cease and the flea never dies.
Where the sun is so hot if in it you remain,
'Twill turn you quite black on your government claim.

How happy am I on my government claim,
Where I've nothing to lose and nothing to gain.
Nothing to eat and nothing to wear,
Nothing from nothing is honest and square.
But here I am stuck and here I must stay,
My money's all gone and I can't get away.
There's nothing will make a man hard and profane,
Like starving to death on a government claim.

Then come to Lane County, there's room for you all,
Where the winds never cease and the rains never fall.

Come join in the chorus and boast of her fame,
While starving to death on your government claim.

Now don't get discouraged, ye poor hungry men,
We're all here as free as a pig in a pen.
Just stick to your homestead and battle your fleas,
And pray to your Maker to send you a breeze.
Now a word to claim holders who are bound for to stay,
You may chew your hardtack till you're toothless and gray.
But as for me, I'll no longer remain,
And starve like a dog on my government claim.

Farewell to Lane County, farewell to the West!
I'll travel back East to the gal I love best.
I'll stop in Missouri and get me a wife,
And live on corn dodgers the rest of my life!

The promise of 160 acres of free land—to be had for the price of living on it for five years—drew many people like the song's Frank Bolar to Kansas in the 1880's. Although the Homestead Act, which opened up the Kansas-Nebraska territory to settlers, was passed in 1862, the rush for land didn't really get into full swing until the '80's.

Early settlers did, in fact, find choice parcels of farm land above the ninety-eighth meridian, which marks a line of abrupt climatic change, separating a temperate zone with good rainfall from a zone of extreme temperatures and little, if any, rain.

Homesteaders like Bolar, who settled in Lane County, Kansas, had no choice but the bad land which was left. On the barren, arid prairies, he and the others built homes out of mud and sod because there was no wood to be found.

In the summer, their crops withered and died in the blistering heat. In the winter, blizzards were commonplace, and large numbers of settlers either froze to death or starved during their first winter. Those who survived did so by burning twists of hay in their stoves; when the hay ran out, they burned the furniture, along with the wagons and anything else which would give a little heat.

In the spring, then, a man like Frank Bolar could wake up one morning to find he had no food, no tools with which to plow, no money to replace his tools, and not even a wagon in which to escape such a living hell.

And if crop failures and constant blizzards weren't enough of a discouragement, there were howling dust storms which raged across the plains for days at a time. In addition, every few years the land was covered with hordes of grasshoppers which not only stripped the prairie of all vegetation but also ate wooden tool handles and the very clothes which the settlers wore.

Bolar, who pieced this song together from the tattered bits of his deflated dream, was one of the many homesteaders who gave up and headed back East, poor but still alive.

Sometimes I Feel Like a Motherless Child

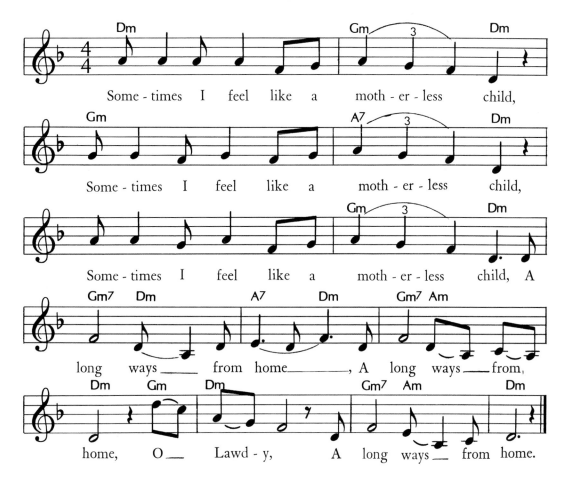

Sometimes I feel like I has no friend,
Sometimes I feel like I has no friend,
Sometimes I feel like I has no friend,
And a long ways from home, a long ways from home,
O Lawdy, a long ways from home.

Sometimes I feel like I'm almost gone,
Sometimes I feel like I'm almost gone,
Sometimes I feel like I'm almost gone,
And a long ways from home, a long ways from home,
O Lawdy, a long ways from home.

Another black spiritual whose exact story has been lost to the ages, this song expresses a sentiment which is not hard to understand. Even without knowing the circumstances surrounding its composition, the power of its lyrics come though to any contemporary singer.

Its three short verses eloquently express a down-and-out feeling of loneliness and despair which all of us, at one time or another, have had to wrestle with.

Navajo Happiness Song

Shee_____ na sha, shee_____na sha,

shee_____ na sha - na nay na no na nay na nay na da.

Na - na na - da no na no, Na - na na - da no na sha.—

The "happiness" reflected in this song is more an emotional expression of pained relief than joyful exaltation. This song came out of a period when the culture of the Navajos, as well as that of the other American Indian tribes, was in its death throes at the hands of merciless white military men.

The real beginning of this song was when Union General James J. Carleston was sent to attack a Confederate force in Texas in 1862. Carleston arrived to find that the Southern army he was supposed to attack had retreated months before. Stranded in New Mexico with nothing to do, Carleston's men were put to work building roads or guarding the mail. During that time, the general became the subject of a blistering series of newspaper articles ridiculing the idleness of his troops during wartime.

With no Confederate force within striking distance, the enraged general declared war on the Indians in the area. Along with ordering his men to attack the Indian villages, General Carleston decreed that all Indian males in the New Mexico-Arizona territory be killed on sight.

In January of 1864—amid glowing press accounts of his bravery in putting down an Indian rebellion—Carleston attacked the main Navajo stronghold in the Canyon of de Chelly. For as long as any Navajo could remember, the canyon, with its sheer red cliffs and towering sandstone pinnacles, had been home.

After waging a successful battle on the unsuspecting Navajos, Carleston marched twenty-four hundred Indian survivors out of the canyon. On foot, they were driven over three hundred miles to Fort Sumner, at the Bosque Rodondo reservation on the Pecos River, where all the male Navajos were imprisoned. Their women and children camped on the reservation, where crop failures and widespread sickness killed many of them. It was during this time that the Happiness Song was first heard.

The Indian women repeated the song over and over again outside the prison where their husbands and sons were kept. The chant was often continued day and night in hopes that the imprisoned men would hear it and take encouragement from its positive rhythm.

In 1868, the Navajos who had survived incarceration and the women and children still alive on the squalid Bosque Rodondo reservation were quietly released by an order from Washington officials. Those officials were said to have been embarrassed by Carleston's apparent bad error in judgment.

Roll Out, Heave Dat Cotton

I hear de bell a-ring-in', I see de cap-tain stand. Boat done blow'd her whis-tle, I know she's gwine to land. I hear de mate a-call-in', "Go git out de plank! Rush out wid de head-line an', tie her to de bank."

Chorus

Roll out, heave dat cot-ton, Roll out, heave dat cot-ton. Roll out, ___ heave dat cot-ton, cot-ton's on its way!

It's early in de mornin', before we see de sun.
Roll aboard dis cotton an' come back in a run.
De captain's in a hurry, I know just what he means,
Wants to beat the *Sherlock* down to New Orleans.

(Refrain)

I hear dat mate a-shoutin', an' see him on de shore.
"Hurry, boys, step lively! Ain' but fifty more.
We ain' got time to tarry around dis cotton pile,
Gwine to git another below here forty mile."

(Refrain)

No collection of American folk songs would be complete without at least one of the tunes which was born on the decks of the great paddle-wheeled river boats. "Roll Out, Heave Dat Cotton" comes from a period in the mid-1800's when cotton may have been king, but the river boats were the queens of America.

Along with the cotton gin, the "wheelers" were largely responsible for revolutionizing the cotton industry. Prior to 1811, cotton barons had to ship their cotton overland or by the slow and cumbersome flatboats down the Mississippi to New Orleans. Profits were mostly eaten up by the cost of transportation. But then the giant river boats came and, in the space of a decade, were soon hauling thousands of tons of cotton at a time from ports all along the Mississippi to Orleans. Cotton delivery was fast, cheap, and relatively dependable.

By 1850, the coal-eating, steam-belching river queens had become the lifeline of a vast portion of the American continent connected by the rivers feeding into the Mississippi. Cities such as St. Louis blossomed almost overnight, and received river boat visits at the rate of five thousand a year.

For all the glamour attributed to river boat life through songs such as this one—as well as through the works of people such as Mark Twain—it was mostly a dreary, dangerous existence. By 1850, when trade on the river was reaching its peak, over five hundred boats had gone to the bottom. The crewmen who lay with them numbered in the many hundreds. Blown boilers were a frequent cause of such catastrophes, but storms, as well as sabotage, played equally important roles.

I Gave My Love a Cherry

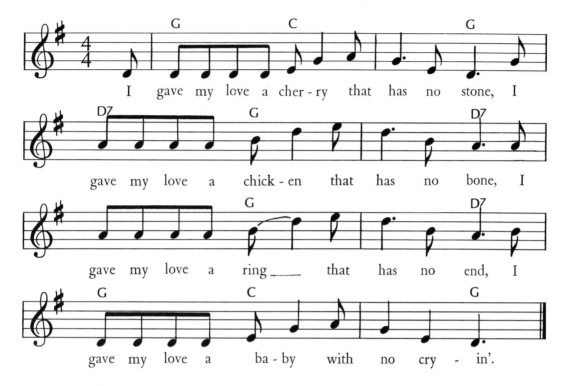

How can there be a cherry that has no stone?
How can there be a chicken that has no bone?
How can there be a ring that has no end?
How can there be a baby with no cryin'?

A cherry when it's bloomin', it has no stone;
A chicken when it's pippin', it has no bone;
A ring when it's rollin', it has no end;
A baby when it's sleepin', it's not cryin'.

This happy ballad, which is almost a riddle, was heard often by the young girls of the old New England colonies. It was a favorite courting song employed by the young men of the area. It is thought to have been first brought to America by the Calvinists, and although the facts surrounding its background have faded, the light and happy mood of its lyrics and melody still remain with us.

The Handcart Song

Ye Saints who dwell on Europe's shore, Prepare yourselves for many more To
For you must cross the raging main Before   the promised land you gain, And

leave be - hind your na - tive land, For sure God's judg - ments are at hand.
with the faith - ful make a start To cross the plains with your hand - cart.

Chorus

For some must push and some must pull, As we go marching up the hill, So

mer - ri - ly   on the way we go, Un - til we reach the val - ley - o.

The lands that boast of modern light,
We know are all as dark as night,
Where poor men toil and want for bread,
Where peasant hosts are blindly led;
These lands that boast of liberty
You ne'er again would wish to see,
When you from Europe make a start
To cross the plains with your handcart.

(Chorus)

This song, which is now remembered as a high-spirited Mormon recruiting song, first
came into being during one of the most disastrous periods in that religion's development.

In 1847, fleeing persecution in the East, Brigham Young and his small band of
Mormon followers established a settlement in Utah. In little less than a decade, the
frugal and industrious Mormons had turned the semidesert lands into lush farm fields.
Abundant crops and huge herds of cattle became the basis of a self-sustaining Mormon
financial empire.

With expansionist visions, Young set up the machinery for a vigorous recruiting campaign. Roaming Europe, missionaries enticed converts by the thousands to emigrate to Utah. Not only was the price of their transatlantic voyage paid by a special Mormon Emigration Fund but the fund also supplied train fare to Iowa City, and a wagon and supplies for the last fourteen hundred miles of the journey.

In 1855, however, disaster struck the Mormon settlement. Crops were wiped out by hordes of grasshoppers. In addition, the winter that year was unexplainably severe. Blizzards of unprecedented strength and duration killed almost all the Mormon cattle. By the spring, Young's followers had no food, cattle, or money. The financial base of the community had been destroyed, and the Emigration Fund was nearly bankrupt. Meanwhile, two thousand European emigrants were in Iowa City awaiting the promised transportation to Utah.

In desperation, and no longer able to provide the customary wagons, Young ordered that the waiting converts be supplied with cheap handcarts and told them they would have to walk to Utah.

Bundling their belongings and meager supplies onto the flimsy carts, the emigrants set out across the desert. In short order, the carts—which had been constructed from green wood—began to dry and warp from the heat of the sun. The desert sand caused their wooden axles to grind away and finally fall apart. The handcarters ran out of food and many starved; cholera swept their ranks killing many others; and an unexpected freak blizzard killed one-fifth of those that were left.

The handful of survivors who finally made it to Utah would later sing "The Handcart Song" as a satiric jab at the "free" journey they had enjoyed. The song was later picked up and taken to Europe by zealous recruiters who made handcart journeys sound like the ultimate in modern travel.

Lowly Bethlehem

Not Jerusalem, lowly Bethlehem, 'twas
That gave us Christ to save us,
Not Jerusalem, favored Bethlehem,
Honored is that name. Thence came
Jesus to release us,
Favored Bethlehem.

This tune about lowly Bethlehem was written in the 1700's, and the town in question was not where Christ was born but rather the city in Pennsylvania which is now a major steel center.

Bethlehem, in Pennsylvania's Northhampton County, was originally established by members of the Church of the Society of United Brethren. This religious sect, under the leadership of Nicholas Ludwig, Count of Zenzendorf, fled persecution in Germany and traveled to America. After unsuccessfully trying to settle in a number of locations, Ludwig finally took his followers into a remote section of Pennsylvania. A particularly industrious people, the Brethren had a prosperous farming community under way within a year's time.

At a meeting called to decide on a name for their new town, many of the Brethren wanted to call it Jerusalem. Ludwig, however, insisted on the name Bethlehem, pointing

out that "Not Jerusalem, lowly Bethlehem 'twas that gave us Christ to save us." The words spoken by Ludwig during that debate were later put to music by one of his faithful, and the tune was sung often in the Pennsylvania town.

Blow the Man Down

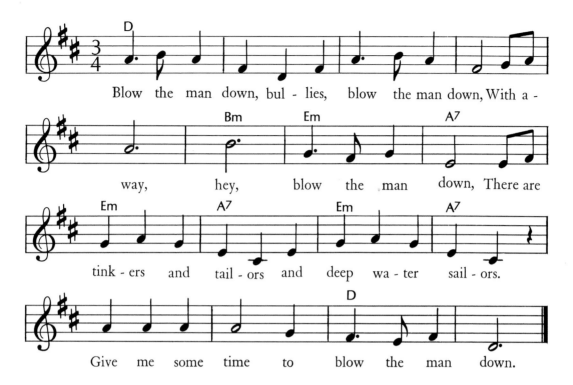

Blow the man down, bul - lies, blow the man down, With a -
way, hey, blow the man down, There are
tink - ers and tail - ors and deep wa - ter sail - ors.
Give me some time to blow the man down.

'Twas on board a Black Baller I first served my time,
And away, hey, blow the man down.
And on the Black Baller I wasted my prime.
Give me some time to blow the man down.

It's when a Black Baller's preparing for sea,
And away, hey, blow the man down
You'd split your sides laughing at the sights you would see,
Give me some time to blow the man down.

With the tinkers and tailors and soldiers and all,
And away, hey, blow the man down.
That ship as good seamen on board the Black Ball.
Give me some time to blow the man down.

It's when a Black Baller is clear of the land,
And away, hey, blow the man down.
Our boatswain [bosun] then gives us the word of command.
Give me some time to blow the man down.

"Lay aft!" is the cry "to the break of the poop!"
And away, hey, blow the man down.
"Or I'll help you along with the toe of my boot."
Give me some time to blow the man down.

It's larboard and starboard on the deck you will sprawl,
And away, hey, blow the man down.
For "Kicking Jack Williams" commands the Black Ball.
Give me some time to blow the man down.

Pay attention to orders, yes, you, one and all,
And away, hey, blow the man down.
For see right above you there flies the Black Ball.
Give me some time to blow the man down.

It's when a Black Baller comes down to the dock,
And away, hey, blow the man down.
The lasses and lads to the pierheads do flock.
Give me some time to blow the man down.

International sea trade underwent a dramatic revolution in 1816, with the establishment of the "Black Ball Line." So named for the large black ball insignia on their sails, the sleek packet ships offered the first system of regularly scheduled ocean voyages between New York and major world ports. Previously, commercial cargoes had to be routed at the convenience of whatever ships were on hand at the time.

The new Black Ballers caused an overnight explosion in ocean trade as merchants discovered the high profit margin and increased market potential offered by such systematic cargo routing. In less than a decade, those same merchants owned and operated almost all the major shipping lines which had sprung up to compete with the immensely successful Black Ball.

Ship captains soon became kingpins in the system, where financial success depended almost solely on a ship's ability to arrive at an appointed port on time, despite wind conditions, weather problems, or crew shortages. Along with high salaries, captains commanded fat commissions on their cargoes. And the faster their ships arrived, the richer and more famous they became.

As the rigors of the ocean voyages became increasingly harsh, crewmen became proportionately scarce. To fill out crews depleted by ship jumpers, captains retained the services of professional "crimpers" who roamed the waterfront using clubs and fists to "recruit" able-bodied men.

To "blow the man down" was waterfront jargon meaning to bash the individual a good one, and then haul him away to the ship's hold. These hapless "tinkers, tailors, and soldiers" mentioned in the song only regained consciousness once they were miles out at sea. Captains such as notorious "Kicking Jack Williams" then used whips, marlin spikes, boot heels, and similar forms of torture to force the shanghied greenhorns to do the ship's work.

Pat Works on the Railway

In eight-een hun-dred and for-ty-one, I
put me cor-du-roy brit-ches on, I put me cor-du-roy
brit-ches on. To work up—on the rail-way.

Chorus

Fi - li - me oo - re oo - re - ay, Fi - li - me oo - re
oo - re - ay, Fi - li - me oo - re
oo - re - ay, To work up - on the rail - way.

In eighteen hundred and forty-two,
I left the old world for the new,
Bad cess to the luck that brought me through
To work upon the railway.

(Chorus)

When we left Ireland to come here,
And spend our latter days in cheer,
Our bosses, they did drink strong beer
And we worked on the railway.

(Chorus)

115

Our contractor's name it was Tom King,
He kept a store to rob the men,
A Yankee cheat with ink and pen
To cheat Pat on the railway.

(Chorus)

It's "Pat, do this," and "Pat, do that!"
Without a stocking or a hat,
And nothing but an old cravat
While Pat works on the railway.

(Chorus)

One Monday morning to our surprise,
Just half an hour before sunrise,
The dirty devil went to the skies
And Pat worked on the railway.

(Chorus)

This song is the sad lament of the countless Irish immigrants who entered this country in the 1840's searching for a quick fortune. Instead of easy wealth, however, they found hostility, sickness, and wide unemployment.

What began as a modest flow of Irish immigrants in 1840 had turned into a flood by 1845, when the potato famine caused tens of thousands of Irish farmers to seek an alternative life. In America they found themselves squeezed out of meaningful jobs by the vicious anti-Irish sentiments which raged across the country. Once again facing the same threat of starvation which had initially brought them to America, the Irishmen gravitated to the railroad yards. There, out of desperation, these seasoned hard laborers worked for poverty wages.

There was little joy in the life of a man laying track for the Union or Central Pacific. The bewildered and disoriented laborers were liberally taken advantage of by greedy railroad bosses. Often they weren't paid; when they were, large chunks of their salaries were siphoned off by the high prices at the company store. The harsh realities of life for these railroad men could have provided bitter lyrics for a hundred such songs.

Sioux Indians

I'll sing you a song, though it may be a sad one,___ Of
tri - als_____ and trou - bles and where first be - gun;
_____ I left my dear fam-'ly, my___ friends and my home___ To
cross the wide moun - tains and des - erts to roam.___

I crossed the Missouri and joined a large train,
Which bore us over mountains, through valley and plain;
And often of an evening a-hunting we'd go
To shoot the fleet antelope and wild buffalo.

We heard of Sioux Indians all out on the plains,
A-killing poor drivers and burning their trains,
A-killing poor drivers with arrows and bows;
When captured by Indians no mercy they'd show.

We traveled three weeks till we come to the Platte,
A-pitching our tents at the head of the flat;
We spread down our blankets on the green shady ground
Where the mules and the horses were grazing around.

While taking refreshment, we heard a loud yell,
The whoop of Sioux Indians come up from the dell.
We sprang to our rifles with a flash in each eye,
And says our brave leader, "We'll fight till we die."

They made a bold dash and they come near our train;
The arrows fell around us like showers of rain,

But with our long rifles we fed them hot lead,
Till many a brave warrior around us lay dead.

We shot their bold chief at the head of their band,
He died like a warrior with his bow in his hand.
When they saw their brave chief lie dead in his gore,
They whooped and they yelled and we saw them no more.

In our little band there were just twenty-four,
And of the Sioux Indians five hundred or more;
We fought them with courage, we spoke not a word,
The whoop of Sioux Indians was all could be heard.

We hooked up our horses and started our train;
Three more bloody battles this trip on the plain.
And in our last battle three of our brave boys fell,
And we left them to rest in the green shady dell.

In virtually all the Indian-related songs such as this one, composed by white settlers in the frontier days, the lyrics dwell on the barbarisms of the redman but never hint at the source of those animosities. The Sioux, in both song and story, have been celebrated for the ferociousness with which they fought the Caucasian settlers traveling through their land in the 1800's.

At one time, the Sioux ruled a vast section of America which included the lands drained by the Missouri, White, and Teton rivers. First contacted by Louis and Clark on their famous expedition, the Indians remained on good terms with whites for nearly forty-five years.

Then the great push West began. Whites, such as the writer of this song, swarmed across Indian lands, contemptuously disregarding all the sacred Sioux beliefs. Buffalo were slaughtered, other game scattered, and the redmen were treated as trespassers on the land where they had lived for hundreds of years.

The wagon trains which zigzagged across the Sioux lands also brought strange diseases such as smallpox with them. Never before exposed to smallpox, the Indians had no defenses against the disease, and they died in droves. Bewildered, the Sioux watched as entire villages were wiped out by the sicknesses of the white man. It was then that they opened their campaign to stem the tide of covered wagons. In the end, innumerable thousands of both Indians and whites wound up at "rest in the green shady dell."

Marines' Hymn

Here's health to you and to our Corps
Which we are proud to serve;
In many a strife we've fought for life
And never lost our nerve.
If the Army and the Navy
Ever look on heaven's scenes,
They will find the streets are guarded
By United States Marines!

This song, to which millions of feet have pounded parade grounds, was written by an anonymous Marine.

Its lyrics tell of the earliest skirmishes in which the Marines fought, including the Mexican War ("halls of Montezuma"), and the battles against the Barbary Coast pirates ("shores of Tripoli").

Those battles gave the Marines an international reputation, and subsequent involvements in the Civil War, at such places as Belleau Wood, put the Corps on a par with the country's other military forces.

The Corps, as the song implies, prides itself on its fierceness and, even today, remains in constant competition with the other services.

The Dreary Black Hills

Kind folks, you will pit-y my hor-ri-ble tale; I'm an
ob-ject that's need-y and look-ing quite stale. I
gave up my trade, sell-ing Wright's Pat-ent Pills, To go
dig-ging for gold in the drear-y Black Hills.

Chorus

Don't go a-way, stay at home if you can, Far a-
way from that cit-y, they call it Chey-enne, For
old Sit-ting Bull and Co-man-che Bill Will
raise up your hair in the drear-y Black Hills.

In Cheyenne the Round House is filled up every night
With Pilgrims of every description in sight;

No clothes on their backs, in their pockets no bills,
And yet they are striking out for the Black Hills.

(Chorus)

When I came to the Black Hills, no gold could I find,
I thought of the free lunch I left far behind;
Through rain, hail, and sleet, nearly froze to the gills,
They call me the orphan boy of the Black Hills.

(Chorus)

Oh, I wish that the man who first started this sell
Was a captive, and Crazy Horse had him in—well,
There is no use in grieving or swearing like pitch,
But the man who would stay here is a son of a —.

(Chorus)

So now to conclude, this advice I'll unfold,
Don't come to the Black Hills a-looking for gold.
For Big Wallapie and Comanche Bill
Are scouting, I'm told, in the dreary Black Hills.

(Chorus)

The Black Hills gold rush, which rolled across the sacred grounds of the Sioux, leaving behind a carpet of boom towns and graveyards in the 1870's, was the result of a carefully planned hoax. This song tells the story of what the gold hunters really found when they went to the Black Hills. Along with no gold, they found no food, and often no way out of the treacherous valleys and canyons.

Wildly exaggerated rumors of vast gold deposits in the region began to circulate in 1874 after a brief mention of gold was found in the diary of Father Peter John De Smet. De Smet, who was permitted to visit the sacred Indian land of "Paha-Sapa," at one time was shown a few grains of gold dust by a Sioux chief.

In the same year that De Smet died and his diary was read, a depression spread across the country. Banks and large industries like the railroads found themselves in serious financial trouble. Ways of pumping some life back into the economy were desperately sought.

Acting in apparent collusion with government officials, executives of the Northern Pacific Railroad decided to create a "gold discovery," and did so with properly placed press releases.

Helping to reinforce rumors, General Custer was sent to camp in the Indian land of the Black Hills. Newspaper stories—allegedly written even before Custer left on the sortie—made a big point of the fact that the general entered the Indian land accompanied by two naturalists, a geologist, and two veteran gold miners.

Needing no further prompting, the gold rush began and the Northern Pacific hauled prospectors by the thousands to the country of the Black Hills. Towns such as Cheyenne, Wyoming, sprang up in the space of weeks. But within three years the "rush" collapsed when no large deposits of gold were found.

The disillusionment of the Black Hills miners was told over and over again in such songs as "The Dreary Black Hills," and can be found in other forms in such places as the Adams Museum in Deadwood, South Dakota, where a preserved limestone slab reads "Came to these hills . . . seven of us . . . all ded but me . . . killed by Indians beyond the high hill . . . I have lost my gun and nothing to eat . . . Indians hunting me."

Nancy Till

Down in the cane - brake, close by the mill

There lived a yel - low girl, her name was Nan - cy Till. She

knew that I loved her, she knew it long, I'm

go in' to ser - e - nade her and I'll sing __ this __ song.

Chorus

Come, love, come, the boat lies low, She

lies __ high and dry on the O - hi - o,

Come, love, come, won't you come a - long with me?

I'll take you down to Ten - nes - see.

Sung by a lovesick keelboat man, this ballad came out of the settlements along the muddy Ohio River. Nancy Till, no doubt, refused the offer to accompany her suitor down to Tennessee—and with good reason. Keelboat crews were infamous for their bad manners. The last place any woman would possibly want to be was along an isolated stretch of river with a group of drunken rivermen at night.

Like rivermen everywhere, keelboaters often sought to replace the women left behind with songs about them. Singing was an integral part of a boatman's life, partly because it helped to soothe those stretches of loneliness and partly because it helped him forget the hellish job he had to face each morning.

Keelboating was the crudest form of river travel. Little more than awkward square barges, the boats were loaded with their cargoes, then poled down the river. When the river became deeper, the barges had to be pulled from the shore. If trees, rocks, or shrubs along the shore prohibited such pulling, they had to be cut down, scaled, or burned off, respectively.

Keelboats sank or overturned with alarming regularity; and even if everything went right with the boat, there was still the possibility of Indian raids or fights with crews of rival boat companies.

In light of the hardships of their work, it is not surprising that so many boatmen took to singing and sought to lose themselves and their troubles for a short while in the lyrics and melodies of such songs as "Nancy Till."

The Drunkard's Doom

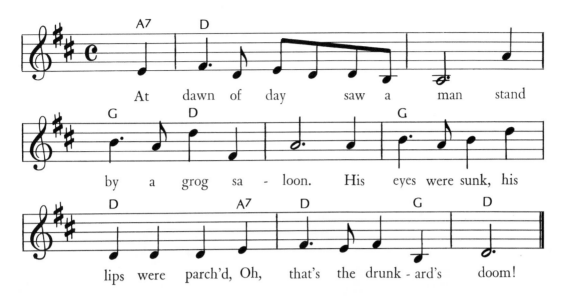

At dawn of day saw a man stand by a grog sa - loon. His eyes were sunk, his lips were parch'd, Oh, that's the drunk - ard's doom!

His little son stood by his side
And to his father said,
"Father, Mother lies sick at home
And Sister cries for bread."

He rose and staggered to the bar
As oft he'd done before,
And to the landlord softly said,
"Just fill me one glass more."

The cup was filled at his command,
He drank of the poisoned bowl,
He drank, while wife and children starved,
And ruined his own soul.

A year had passed; I went that way,
A hearse stood at the door.
I paused to ask and one replied,
"The drunkard is no more."

I saw the hearse move slowly on,
No wife or child was there,
They, too, had flown to heaven's bright home
And left a world of care.

Now all young men, a warning take
And shun the poisoned bowl.

'Twill lead you down to hell's dark gate
And ruin your own soul.

Contemporary singers of this morbid tune can thank the fine ladies of the Women's Christian Temperance Union for their material. "The Drunkard's Doom" has the distinction of being one of the extremely few antialcohol songs ever written by an American composer.

A direct result of the temperance movement, which steamed into existence in the 1870's, this song was wailed loudly at the WCTU meetings, as well as outside the saloons which drew that organization's disfavor. One of the loudest and most adamant of the singers was Carrie Nation, a woman who had the unsettling habit of breaking up quiet afternoon drinking parties with an axe.

By 1875, Carrie Nation had chopped her way into the national spotlight and was paying her frequent court fines by selling souvenir hatchets to sympathizers. With a large national following, the spirited woman continued to sing her songs and perfect ever better ways of splintering a bar. The stink she and the WCTU raised about liquor was instrumental in laying the foundation for the legislation which gave us the disastrous period of national prohibition.

Cowboy Lullaby

Sil - ver sage a - set - tin' in the pale twi - light,

Coy - ote yap - pin' la - zy on the hill,

Sleep - y winks of light a - long the far sky - line,

Time for mill - in' cat - tle to be still.

Chorus

So now, the light - nin's far a - way, The

coy - ote's noth - in' skee - ry, he's sing - in' for his dear - y.

Ya - ho, a cow - boy hol - i - day, So

set - tle down you cat - tle till the morn - in'.

Nothin' out there on the plains that you folks need,
Nothin' there that seems to take your eye.

135

Still you got to watch them or they'll all stampede,
Plungin' down some arroyo bank to die.

(Chorus)

Of all the potential dangers a prairie cowboy had to face, none was more terrifying than the one which came from above. More than Indian raids, rustlers, or rattlesnakes, a cowboy feared lightning.

Thunderstorms, which could rage up with little or no notice on the plains, were the major cause of cattle stampedes. Disoriented, and driven into a wild, frenzied flight by the lightning, stampeding herds of long-horned steers trampled many a horse and sleeping cowboy to death.

In an attempt to keep the steers calm when thunderstorms threatened, cowboys would often sing loudly and in unison to the herd. One cowpuncher composed the "Cowboy Lullaby" in 1881 for this purpose, and it caught on quickly to become the common song of the night cattle watch.

Often sensing the approach of an electrical storm before it was even visible, the steers would begin to mill in circles. Cowboys on night watch would circle the milling herd and begin singing. Sometimes, if the storm did not pass directly overhead, the gentle, lulling rhythm of the tune would keep the cattle hovering just this side of a stampede.

The Buffalo Skinners

'Twas in the town of Jacks - bo - ro in the spring of sev - en - ty - three, A man by the name of Cre - go __ came step - ping up to me, __ Say - ing, "How do you do, young fel - low, __ and how would you like to go __ And spend one sum - mer pleas - ant - ly on the range of the buf - fa - lo?"

It's me being out of employment, this to Crego I did say,
"This going out on the buffalo range depends upon the pay.
But if you will pay good wages and transportation too,
I think, sir, I will go with you to the range of the buffalo."

"Yes, I will pay good wages, give transportation too,
Provided you will go with me and stay the summer through;
But if you should grow homesick, come back to Jacksboro,
I won't pay transportation from the range of the buffalo."

It's now our outfit was complete, seven able-bodied men,
With navy six and needle gun, our troubles did begin;

Our way it was a pleasant one, the route we had to go,
Until we crossed Pease River on the range of the buffalo.

It's now we've crossed Pease River, our troubles have begun.
The first damned tail I went to rip, Christ! how I cut my thumb!
While skinning the damned old stinkers our lives they had no show,
For the Indians watched to pick us off while skinning the buffalo.

He fed us on such sorry chuck I wished myself most dead
It was old jerked beef, croton coffee, and sour bread.
Pease River's as salty as hell fire, the water I could never go,
O God! I wished I had never come to the range of the buffalo.

Our meat it was buffalo hump and iron wedge bread,
And all we had to sleep on was a buffalo robe for a bed;
The fleas and gray-backs worked on us, O boys, it was not slow,
I'll tell you there's no worse hell on earth than the range of the buffalo.

Our hearts were cased with buffalo hocks, our souls were cased with steel
And the hardships of that summer would nearly make us reel.
While skinning the damned old stinkers our lives they had no show,
For the Indians waited to pick us off on the hills of Mexico.

The season being near over, old Crego he did say
The crowd had been extravagant, was in debt to him that day;
We coaxed him and we begged him and still it was no go,
We left old Crego's bones to bleach on the range of the buffalo.

Oh, it's now we've crossed Pease River and homeward we are bound,
No more in that hell-fired country shall ever we be found.
Go home to our wives and sweethearts, tell others not to go,
For God's forsaken the buffalo range and the damned old buffalo.

During the latter part of the 1800's, the buffalo skinners left a highly visible trail as they roamed the North American continent. From Canada to southern Texas, the skinners left behind vast buffalo bone yards which often stretched as far as the eye could see across sections of the Great Plains.

Their grisly trade took hold as a national passion in the 1870's when Eastern fashion centers took a fancy to buffalo-hide garments, and Eastern leather factories developed efficient methods of treating large numbers of the raw animal hides.

Drawing a fee of three dollars per hide from the factories, men such as Crego led swarms of skinners West, and, in a little over a quarter of a century, slaughtered nearly fifty million of the great, shaggy beasts. Armed with .55-caliber Sharps rifles, buffalo hunters could easily cut down a running animal at fifteen hundred yards. A few such well-armed men could kill a herd of hundreds in a day's time. The beast's skin was then sliced from its body and the carcass left to rot.

At the height of the craze, the railroads provided special buffalo runs which carted tons of animal skins at a time from plains depots such as Dodge City, Kansas, to the Eastern factories.

Although lucrative, the skinner's profession involved a great deal of physical risk, and it was not unusual for men like Crego to meet their death on the plains. If not killed by greedy companions, they were likely to fall prey to the hazards of the rugged terrain or become victims of Indian warriors who saw no sport in the wanton slaughter of the great buffalo herds.

In the Evening by the Moonlight

In the evening by the moonlight you can hear those voices singing. In the
evening by the moonlight you can hear those banjoes ringing! How the
old folks would enjoy it! They would sit all night and listen. As we
sang in the eve - ning by the moon - light.
Hear those bells! Don't you hear those bells? They are
ring - ing out the glo - ry of the Lamb.
Hear those bells! Don't you hear those bells? They are
ring - ing out the glo - ry of the Lamb.

Sung often from the porches of the huge plantation mansions which studded the South,
this is one of the romantic songs recalling the splendors of the ante-bellum era.

Back when cotton was king, residents of the opulent mansions spent many nights

amusing themselves with such songs. With the hovels of their slave workers hidden from view by sumptuous hedges of magnolia and azalea, plantation owners would sing of life's inherent beauty. The atmosphere of the times never forced them to scrutinize the incongruity between the lyrics of songs they sang and the actual life they led.

Two Little Children

Two lit-tle chil-dren, a boy and a girl, Sat down by an old church door; The lit-tle girl's feet were as brown as the curl That fell on the dress that she wore.

The little boy's coat was all ragged and torn;
A tear shone in each little eye.
"Why don't you run home to your mamma?" I said,
And this was the maiden's reply:

"Mama got sick. Angels took her away,"
She said, "to a home warm and bright.
She said she would come for her darlings some day.
Perhaps she is coming tonight."

"Papa was lost on the sea long ago;
We waited all night on the shore.
He was a lifesaving captain, you know,
But he never came back any more."

The sexton came early to ring the church bell
And found them beneath the snow white.
The angels had made room for the darlings to dwell
In heav'n with their mother that night.

Although the exact origin and circumstances of "Two Little Children" are unknown, the song could well be an anthem to the children who died by the scores on the frontier.

They were the first to succumb to the ravages of disease and malnutrition, as well as the group most susceptible to the cold and the heat.

Of all the graves on which America was built, none are sadder than those of the innocent youngsters who never lived to understand the things for which they were dying.

Old Blue

I raised a dog an his name was Blue, And I bet-cha five
dol-lars he's a good one too. "Go on, Blue, I'm com-in'
too. Go on, Blue, I'm com-in' too."

Shouldered my axe and tooted my horn,
Gonna get me a possum in the new ground corn.
"Go on, Blue, I'm comin' too. Go on, Blue, I'm comin' too."

Old Blue treed, I went to see,
There sat the possum in a 'simmon tree.
"Go on, Blue, I'm comin' too."
"Go on, Blue, I'm comin' too."

Possum clumb down on a swingin' limb
Blue barked at the possum, possum growled at him.
"Go on, Blue, you good dawg you. Go on, Blue, you good dawg you."

Although written near the end of the Revolutionary War, "Old Blue" is a song that can still strike a melancholy chord in anyone who has suffered the loss of a favorite dog. The sad tune was initially composed on the ukelele of Tim Cathcart, a soldier in the Colonial army.

Cathcart, cut off from his battalion and hiding from the British in dense woods, came upon an old dog which was injured and near death from starvation. Despite the dangers inherent in staying in any one place for more than a few hours, Cathcart camped for days and nursed the dog back to health. Meanwhile, British troops continued to comb the woods and often passed within talking distance of the soldier's camp.

The dog recovered quickly and he and Cathcart became inseparable, often sharing the same food as well as sleeping quarters. Cathcart picked the name Blue because of the many subtle hues of that color which he saw in the dog's ebon coat. Blue faithfully stayed with his master for many months after the soldier rejoined his unit.

One day while hunting, the dog was attacked and gored to death by a vicious possum. Deeply grieved over the loss, Cathcart sang this song night after night over the company campfire. Other soldiers who had lost dogs were moved by the lyrics and sang them frequently, so that soon the tune spread throughout the colonies.

A La Ru

Duér - me - te, Ni - ño lin - do,_____ En los bra - zos dei_____ a - mor Mien - tras que duer - me y des - can - sa_____ La pe - na de mi do - lor.

Chorus
A la ru,_____ a la me,_____ A la ru,_____ a la me, A la ru,_____ a la me,_____ A la ru, a la ru, a la me.

(Oh sleep, Thou Holy Baby,
With Thy head against my breast;
Meanwhile the pangs of my sorrow
Are soothed and put to rest.)

(Chorus)

No temas al rey Herodes
Que nada te ha de hacer;
En los brazos de tu madre
Y ahi nadie te ha de ofender.

(Thou need'st not fear King Herod,
He will bring no harm to you;

So rest in the arms of your mother
Who sings You a la ru.)

(Chorus)

A Spanish lullaby to Jesus, "A La Ru" came into the pages of American folklore as part of the rich heritage of our Mexican-American population.

This song, which was originally part of a Christmas play, dates back to the 1500's and can still be heard in contemporary religious ceremonies in many Southwestern states.

The Indian civilizations of what is now Mexico did not take kindly to the Spanish armies which came ashore in the 1500's looking for gold. Enslaved and otherwise abused by the Spanish, the Indians steadfastly refused to embrace the principles of European religion.

Zealous Franciscan friars arrived by the boatload, however, and began to circulate through the Indian villages and towns. Frustrated, and occasionally killed, by hostile Indians, the friars began to back up their rosary beads with ranks of well-armed troops. Widespread conversions then began to occur.

In 1852, one of those proselytizing friars was leading a large band of colonizers and missionaries through a small Indian town near the Rio Grande. In the throes of an extended drought, the villagers challenged the padre to ask his god for rain. By a stroke of uncanny luck, the priest's prayers were shortly followed by a steady shower. Awed, the village inhabitants enthusiastically attended the Christmas play which the friar and his followers staged that night.

During that first ceremony of Los Pastores, "A La Ru" was sung, much the same as it continues to be sung now each Christmas.

The text for this book was set in Granjon
by H. O. Bullard, Typographers, New York.
The color separations and printing were done by
Vernon Martin Associates, Inc., Lancaster, Pennsylvania.
The music has been edited, arranged and drawn by Deena Jaworski.